THE MYSTERY
OF JESUS, JEW, AND GENTILE

TYLER WITTENBROOK

Copyright © 2021 by Tyler Wittenbrook. All rights reserved.

The views and opinions expressed in this work are those of the author and do not necessarily reflect the views and opinions of Braughler Books LLC.

This book or any portion thereof may not be reproduced or used in any manner whatsoever without the express written permission of the publisher except for the use of brief quotations in a scholarly work or book review. For permissions or further information contact Braughler Books LLC at:

info@braughlerbooks.com

Cover photo: © Jack Kersey

Unless otherwise noted below, scripture references and quotations are from The ESV® Bible (The Holy Bible, English Standard Version®), copyright © 2001 by Crossway, a publishing ministry of Good News Publishers. Used by permission. All rights reserved.

Scripture references and quotations for The Mystery of Judas (pg 25), The Mystery of Barabbas (pg 29) taken from the Holy Scriptures, Tree of Life Version. Copyright © 2014, 2016 by the Tree of Life Bible Society. Used by permission of the Tree of Life Bible Society.

Printed in the United States of America
Published by Braughler Books LLC., Springboro, Ohio

First printing, 2021

ISBN: 978-1-955791-04-5

Library of Congress Control Number: 2021914920

Ordering information: Special discounts are available on quantity purchases by bookstores, corporations, associations, and others. For details, contact the publisher at:

sales@braughlerbooks.com
or at 937-58-BOOKS

For questions or comments about this book, please write to:

info@braughlerbooks.com

Braughler™
Books
braughlerbooks.com

CONTENTS

The Mystery Introduction 1

PART 1 . . . . **5**
The Mystery of Cain and Abel 7
The Mystery of Moses 11
The Mystery of Passover 13
The Mystery of Holiness 17
The Mystery of Steadfast Love 21
The Mystery of Judas 25
The Mystery of Barabbas 29

PART 2 . . . . **33**
The Mystery of Unity 35
Remember the Mystery 39
The Mystery of Christ 43
The Mystery of God's People 47
The Mystery of Jealousy 51
The Mystery of Honor 55
The Glory of the Mystery 59
The Mystery Conclusion 63

About the Author 67

THE MYSTERY INTRODUCTION

My brother's friend once made a funny joke: violence is not the answer; it's the question, and the answer is yes. This was a joke, of course, and not intended to be taken seriously. I mention it because I am presenting a similarly structured statement: The Mystery is not the answer; it's the question, and the answer is Jesus.

Jesus is always the answer. Why do people say this? The answer for the question of The Mystery is Jesus, but not just because it is the church-y answer for every question. In order to fully understand why Jesus is the answer, we must understand the question.

Jesus is the answer, and I have said that the question is The Mystery. What is The Mystery? It is a complex idea, with many connected questions to ask and answer. This book is intended to bring us to ask such questions, that we may truly know that Jesus alone can answer them. We will seek out the answers together, but there is a great deal of depth to The Mystery, and many questions and layers surrounding it have yet to be uncovered. My desire is that this book would be only the beginning of your journey into The Mystery.

Up until now, I have shrouded this idea in even more mystery. Now, finally, is the question with which I will sum up The Mystery: what is God doing?

The Mystery is all about the purposes of God, and includes further questions, such as: what is the Bible all about? What is the purpose of Israel in God's plan? Why did God allow people outside of Israel to be saved? How are we meant to respond to the gospel? What are the roles of Jews and Gentiles (non-Jews) in God's plan?

The answers to these questions can be found in the Apostle Paul's letters, although there is continually more to discover. He summarizes it in this statement: "This mystery is that the Gentiles are fellow heirs, members of the same body, and partakers of the promise in Christ Jesus through the gospel" (Ephesians 3:6). With whom are the Gentiles "fellow heirs"? Israel, of course! God's chosen people, Israel, are the heirs of God. In Christ, however, both Jew and Gentile are fellow heirs. This revelation baffled the world in that day, so it was called a mystery.

Paul continually includes Gentiles and Jews in The Mystery, and he always writes about it to cities where the believers are primarily Gentiles. Therefore, we must understand both "Jew" and "Gentile." Gentiles are simply non-Jews. All of the Bible is centered around Israel, or the Jewish people. The entire Bible was written by Jews, and the story follows Israel. The Gentiles are everybody else. The word "nations" is also used in Scripture to refer to the Gentiles. Some translations use "Greek" instead of "Gentile" in the New Testament, but a more accurate word is "Gentile," also meaning "heathen." In the Bible, the Jews are God's people, and the Gentiles are not. I am a Gentile. Many readers of this book are likely Gentiles.

The relationship between Jews and Gentiles is central to The Mystery. I love the Jews and recognize that they are crucial to God's purposes, so this book will be utilizing Hebrew words, such as *Yeshua*, *Torah*, and *Tanakh*.

Yeshua is the Hebrew name for Jesus. *Yeshua* means "salvation," as He is our savior. Messiah will be used at times in place of

Christ. Instead of "Christ Jesus" you may see "Messiah *Yeshua*." This word, as well as other Hebrew words, including *Torah*, will be italicized.

Torah means teaching, and the *Torah* includes the first five books of the Bible: Genesis, Exodus, Leviticus, Numbers, and Deuteronomy. Most translations of the Bible will reference these five books, but they will translate *Torah* as "Law," though the correct translation is "Teaching."

Tanakh is another important word, closely related to *Torah*. The *Tanakh* is the Hebrew Scriptures, which Christians often call the Old Testament. The *Tanakh* consists of the *Torah* (Teaching), the *Nevi'im* (Prophets), and the *Ketuvim* (Writings). However, at times the word *Torah* is used in reference to the entirety of the Hebrew Scriptures, the *Tanakh*. Our understanding of these terms and the Hebrew language will impact the way we understand the Bible as a whole.

How do you read and understand the Bible? As you read through the Bible, perhaps you think of Sunday school or VeggieTales depictions of the stories. Perhaps you went to Bible school and have a theologically driven perspective. Perhaps you have just started reading the Bible and it is difficult to understand. If you have been reading the Bible with blurry vision, reading glasses, or sunglasses, put on a new pair of frames as you read this book. The Mystery is like a pair of 3-D glasses, opening your eyes to see that the Bible is all about a central story of reconciliation: between God and man; between Jew and Gentile. You may have heard that the Bible all points to the Messiah. It is true that Messiah *Yeshua* is the pivotal character in the story. Paul states that The Mystery is "the mystery of Christ" (Ephesians 3:4). With our 3-D glasses on, we will discover The Mystery of reconciliation, Jesus being at the center.

Jesus declares in Matthew 5:17 that He came to fulfill the *Torah* and the Prophets. All of the *Torah* prophesies about Him. Some passages of Scripture can be secretly "prophetic," pointing to Jesus and to unlocking The Mystery. We're going to look at some of those passages.

The first seven chapters of this book discuss passages of the Bible that I found point to The Mystery. These chapters are in approximate chronological order of where the individual stories appear in Scripture. Each one occurs before the crux of The Mystery, which is the cross. If the crux - the center - of The Mystery is the cross, then how does the *Tanakh* point us to the cross? Each chapter will give you a passage that points to the cross. The idea is that you will see connections as you read it for yourself. The revelation that I share in each chapter will go in depth into The Mystery of the cross in relation to Jews and Gentiles.

Part 2 of The Mystery dives into the passages where Paul explains The Mystery in great depth. These passages are found in the letters to Gentile believers in Rome, Ephesus, and Colossae. Again, start by reading the Bible passage in each chapter, allow God to teach you, then receive from the revelation shared in that chapter. (My recommendation is to take two weeks to read the fourteen chapters of this book. Each day, dive into the Bible passage and the comments I share, meditating on the connections to The Mystery.)

Enjoy, and let me know if you have any questions! This isn't like a small group so it doesn't quite work that way, but you really can email me any questions or comments you have:

tyler.witten.book@gmail.com

PART 1

THE MYSTERY OF CAIN AND ABEL
Genesis 4

Let's give a quick shoutout to all those people who read the introduction! If you skipped it on accident, just go back and read it really quick. It will give you some great context for reading this book. Without further ado, I present to you The Mystery of Cain and Abel.

The story of Cain and Abel, you will see, is quite prophetic in regard to the gospel and The Mystery as described in Paul's letters. The story of these two brothers is similar in some ways to the story of Jacob and Esau, but I want to highlight this story, as it is about the first two brothers.

In the Conclusion of this book, I have included a list of resources that have been very helpful to me, one of those being the One New Man Bible. Some of the insights shared in this chapter are drawn from that particular translation of Scripture.

The first helpful insight is about the reason that Cain's offering was not acceptable to God, in contrast with Abel's offering. Abel gave to the LORD of the first and the best of his flock, whereas Cain did not give the firstfruits of the ground. As you see in Scripture, God instructs His people Israel to sacrifice the best of the flock and the firstfruits of the ground. God desires for His people to submit to Him out of reverence and love, rather than selfishly holding on to what He has given us. The second helpful insight from the One New Man Bible is about Cain's insolence toward God. Cain was not pleasing to God because he did not give God his best offering, and he dishonored the LORD. Such details may help us understand the connection to the relationship between Israel and the nations.

Cain, the firstborn son of Adam and Eve, is representative of Israel, God's firstborn son. The LORD tells Moses in Exodus 4:22, "Israel is My son, My firstborn." For our purposes, Abel will represent the Gentiles, all of those who are not of Israel.

Cain's offering is not pleasing to God, so God rejects him. Throughout Scripture, the LORD tells Israel that He does not delight in offerings or sacrifices, but He wants their heart, their surrender. The Israelites constantly turn away from God, so He allows the Gentiles an opportunity to turn to Him. When the early church — which initially consisted of only Jews — began preaching the gospel to the Gentiles, many turned to the LORD. Thus, it is comparable to Abel's offering. Abel gave an offering to God that was pleasing to Him, and many Gentiles gave God their hearts, a pleasing offering to the LORD.

Cain responded with anger to God's acceptance of Abel. Likewise, Jews who did not accept the Messiah responded with anger toward those Jews who formed a new "sect" with the uncircumcised, unclean Gentiles.

If Cain represents the Jews, and Abel represents the Gentiles, what do we do with the third son to arise in this story? The third son, of course, is Seth. God does not raise Abel to life and have him continue the line of His people. Neither does the Scripture follow the line of Cain as if he was the one God had chosen. Rather, God gives another son, Seth, to Adam and Eve. The next chapter of Genesis details the descendants of Seth, leading to Noah. Thus, this new man, Seth, continues the story of God. What does Seth represent?

The One New Man Bible is a fitting resource for the process of writing this chapter, as Seth represents the One New Man. Paul's letter to the Ephesians explains that God desired to create, out of the Jews and the Gentiles, "One New Man" (Ephesians 2:15). If Cain represents the Jews and Abel represents the Gentiles, Seth represents this "One New Man." Even from the beginning of Scripture, in the story of the first two brothers on earth, God is pointing to His plan for reconciliation between Jew and Gentile. This is The Mystery: God used the story of Cain and Abel to foreshadow His plan for Jew and Gentile to unite in Christ as One New Man.

THE MYSTERY OF MOSES
Hebrews 3

It is so difficult to pick a single passage for you to read about The Mystery of Moses. Honestly, I would have you read the entirety of Exodus, and probably Deuteronomy too. I would love for you to look at the context of the *Torah* as a whole when viewing The Mystery through the lens of Moses. Then, of course, I would have you read at least one of the Gospels, maybe even all four. That is because Moses' life itself is a prophetic reflection of the Messiah.

I will just share some really quick parallels between Moses and Jesus. First and foremost, Moses was sent by God to save His people from bondage (Exodus 3). Jesus was crucified to save all of mankind from the bondage of sin (Mark 10:32-34, John 19, Romans 8:1-3). Moses gave Israel the teaching (*Torah*) of God (Exodus 19-20). Jesus expounded upon the teaching of Moses (Matthew 5-7). Moses met with God in great intimacy on a mountain (Exodus 19, many other places). Jesus went to pray to God on a mountain (Mark 6:46). At one point, Moses came down from the mountain after a revelation of God, and his face was shining gloriously (Exodus 34), similar to the transfiguration of Jesus (Mark 9). Moses performed great signs for God's glory (Exodus 4, 7-10). Jesus performed many signs and wonders (throughout the Gospels). Moses was instructed by God to build Him a tabernacle, a dwelling place (Exodus 25). Jesus is the foundation on which the church, God's present dwelling place, has been built (Matthew 16:13-18, 21:42). Jesus' real name — His Hebrew name — is *Yeshua*, an alternate spelling of Joshua, Moses' successor (Deuteronomy 31). The Mystery of the Passover is the next chapter of this book, and it explores another massive correlation between Moses and Jesus, and the gospel as a whole. I could go on. And I have. I realize that I gave more than a few examples. There are just so many, and I got excited. I can talk about the many similarities between Jesus and Moses, but I want to also highlight the difference.

Moses did not enter the Promised Land with the rest of Israel. He made a mistake, and God did not allow Him to enter. God's purposes are always perfect, so there was a reason that God made that decision. I believe that a reason that Moses did not enter the Promised Land is so that Israel would know that he is not their Savior. God rescued them from the land of Egypt, and only God could come as the promised Messiah. The header for Hebrews 3 in my Bible is "Jesus Greater Than Moses." This is the main takeaway that I want us to have.

Moses prophesied about the coming Messiah, in his words and in his life. But Moses was not the Messiah. Moses could not completely deliver Israel. The Old Covenant, given by God through Moses, could not give life. The sacrifices that God commanded Moses and Israel to give could not fully atone for their sin. This is The Mystery: Moses was a great leader, prophet and man of God, but Jesus is greater, and He fulfilled the prophecy of the Messiah in Moses' life.

THE MYSTERY OF PASSOVER
Exodus 10:21-12:51

Here's the thing: I was originally planning on just taking this passage and sharing the connections — only from looking at the Scripture — to Christ. I have to be honest, though. I love this passage so much and there is so much that I want to talk about, including outside research. That is another important detail to remember: we can find a great multitude of Bible passages that point to The Mystery, but other resources can help us see connections as well.

I think that I will just go in order. In the reading for this chapter, I purposefully included the ninth plague, the plague of darkness, that occurs right before the Passover event. It is really interesting. I spent some time researching possible natural explanations for the plague of darkness, but none were conclusive. The eclipse theory is simply impossible because the longest possible time for a total eclipse is much less than three days, and the land of Egypt was in complete darkness for three days. The eclipse theory also does not explain how there was light in the Israelite homes. I conducted similar research to find an explanation for the darkness preceding Christ's death on the cross and also found inconclusive information. Here's what's beautiful about these two cases of complete darkness: first, the darkness in Egypt lasted three days, and the darkness during the crucifixion lasted three hours. Second, both cases of darkness are soon followed by the sacrifice of the lamb. Let's focus on that detail now.

Following the plague of darkness and Pharaoh's refusal to let the people of Israel leave, God announces the tenth plague. The angel of death comes to kill every firstborn son in the land of Egypt. God instructs the people of Israel to sacrifice a male lamb without blemish and place the blood of the lamb on the doorposts of every home, so that the angel of death may "pass over" them. Thus, the feast is called the Passover. The children of Israel were commanded by God to celebrate this feast for all generations. In fact, God commands Israel numerous times throughout the Old Testament Scriptures to remember how the Lord brought them out of the land of Egypt. Evidently, it was important to God that the people remember the Passover event. Now why would this be?

You may be aware of the main connection that I will make to Christ from this passage. God desired His people to remember this act of redemption because it is a prophecy of the ultimate redemption to come through Jesus. It is the blood of the lamb that kept the people of Israel from death. John the Baptist declares that Jesus is the Lamb of God in John 1:29. He sees Jesus approaching and exclaims: "Behold, the Lamb of God, who takes away the sin of the world!" Jesus came to fulfill the promise of the Passover as His blood saves the people of God from death. This is essentially the gist of this chapter, but there are so many other cool details about the Passover that I am super excited to talk about.

For one, God tells Moses in Exodus 11:9 that Pharaoh will not listen to him, that the wonders of God may be multiplied in the land of Egypt. Throughout the Gospels, you will find that Jesus tells many people — His disciples, Jewish religious leaders, and Pontius Pilate — who He is. He predicts His own death and resurrection. He informs people that He is the Messiah and the

King of the Jews, yet many people do not believe Him. Clearly it was part of God's purpose that people would not listen to Jesus. This was so that, through the crucifixion and resurrection, the wonders of God may be multiplied in the world.

(I encourage you to conduct some of your own research if you are interested in any of these fascinating details. If you would take the time to look it up, you should find that the time of the sacrifice of the lamb on Passover closely aligns with the time that Christ gave up His life on the cross.)

In verse 22 of the twelfth chapter of Exodus, Moses tells the elders of Israel to place blood on "the lintel and the two doorposts." Go find a nearby doorframe. Act as if you are holding something in your hand, like the hyssop that the elders used, and pretend to touch the door frame with it: first the top of the doorframe, then the left doorpost, followed by the right. You should find that the motion is in the form of a cross, similar to the sign of the cross performed in Catholic prayers. I love this little detail that points to the future sacrifice of Christ, the Lamb, on the cross.

Another interesting detail is found in Exodus 12:40-41. The children of Israel were in the land of Egypt for 430 years, until God delivered them. I am sure there were times when some of them may have felt that God abandoned them. From the time of the prophet Malachi to Jesus, there was a time of "silence" from God, where many Jews surely felt abandoned by God. This time is considered to be approximately 400 years, perhaps even closer to 430 years by the time of the crucifixion of Christ. Yet another cool connection to Christ in the story of the Passover.

Finally, I want to point out the fact that this Passover event preceded the crossing over into the Promised Land. Through the blood shed by the Lamb of God on the cross, all those who would follow Him can enter the Promised Land of the presence of God. What a wonderful promise prophesied in this story!

There are numerous incredible details at which we may marvel in the Passover story. Arguably the most important and most celebrated Jewish festival is a clearly prophetic event pointing to the greatest redemption event in all of human history, the center of the story of God. This is The Mystery: God, in His extravagant mercy, delivered His chosen people out of bondage thousands of years ago, simultaneously prophesying His deliverance of all people out of the bondage of sin and death.

THE MYSTERY OF HOLINESS
Isaiah 6:1-7

The Mystery of Holiness, simply put, is this: God is holy. Without Him we are not holy, and with Him we are. To understand this, we must dive into the meaning of this word, "holy." On multiple occasions, in an act of worship and surrender to the LORD, I have found myself crying out or simply repeating "holy, holy, holy." I knew that this was an appropriate act of worship because it resonated with my spirit, but I was not sure why. I decided to look into it some more and ask God for revelation.

Many of us have heard a definition of the word "holy" along the following lines: "set apart," "sacred," "different," etc. What does this really mean, though? Michael Reeves, in his book *Delighting in the Trinity*, proposes that God "is not set apart from us in priggishness, but by the fact that there are no such ugly traits in him as there are in us." So then, the holiness of God is not an arrogance, pretentiousness, or harshness as some may believe. In fact, the holiness and love of God are not contradictory or separate, as many suppose. One might consider the holiness of God to be the cause of His wrath towards humanity, whereas the love of God is the cause of His grace toward people, counteracting the harshness of His holy wrath. This could not be further from the truth. Love is not a side of God, as 1 John 4:8 states that "God is love." Likewise, holy is not merely a side of God, as in Leviticus 19:2 the LORD says of himself: "I am holy." Rather, as Alec Motyer explains in his commentary on Isaiah, the holiness of God "is the total truth about God." It is the foundation of His being.

"Holy" is the perfect word to describe the nature of God. If God were not holy, He would not be love. He would not be grace, truth, life, beauty, or even good if He were not holy. As Reeves explained, there is nothing ugly or bad about God, and that is what it means to be holy. Thus, every other aspect of His good character cannot be separated from His holiness. This simple word, "holy," encompasses the entirety of His being, and the declaration of it is proper worship to God.

Therefore, the angels around the throne of God constantly declare His praise in the following way, according to Isaiah 6: "Holy, holy, holy is the Lord of hosts; the whole earth is full of his glory!" At first glance, the threefold repetition of this word, "holy," may seem insignificant. As a matter of fact, the rule of three is an effective and common rhetorical device. Preachers also tend to group information into chunks of three. The number three does not necessarily seem to have any particular significance in this passage. Most Christians understand the Biblical motif of three — the Holy Trinity is the most glaring example — and the word "holy" looks to follow that pattern in this passage.

However, "holy, holy, holy" actually breaks a Biblical pattern. There are multiple situations in which a quality may be repeated a second time, or raised to the power of two, in order to suggest a superlative or emphasize the quality. According to Motyer's commentary of Isaiah, this passage is actually the only case in the entire Hebrew Bible in which a quality is raised to the power of three — a "super-superlative" — meaning that, according to Motyer, "the divine holiness is so far beyond anything the human mind can grasp." Thus, the threefold declaration of "holy, holy,

holy" is an act of worship to the God that surpasses understanding.

In fact, this God so surpasses our understanding that the most beautiful word to describe His gospel of holiness is "mystery." That brings us back to the beginning of this chapter, because The Mystery of God is about holiness. The Isaiah 6 passage wonderfully summarizes the mysterious gospel of the LORD's holiness. We see that God is holy, the seraphim worship the LORD in His holiness, and Isaiah's eyes are opened to the holiness of God. Rightfully, his response is humility. He is humbled and recognizes his need for the LORD. God's response is astonishing and quite mysterious. He sends one of the seraphim to take a burning coal from the altar, place it on Isaiah's lips, and declare his atonement. In the presence of God's holiness, Isaiah responds with humility and is made holy.

This is The Mystery of Christ. In Christ, the atonement and holiness that Isaiah receives is made possible. In Christ, we are made holy! Only God is good, and we are not good if separate from Him. But thanks be to God, for the old, ugly, fleshly nature is dead, and we have been raised to new life, to perfect life, to holy life, in Christ! This is The Mystery: God is holy, and He provided a way that we could be holy and be in holy relationship with Him.

THE MYSTERY OF STEADFAST LOVE
Psalm 106

This psalm begins with praise, and it begins with praising the LORD specifically because "his steadfast love endures forever" (v. 1). The psalm continues with this confession: "both we and our fathers have sinned; we have committed iniquity; we have done wickedness" (v. 6), and the following verses proceed to recount the history of the wickedness of the people of Israel. However, this psalm is not about confession. Neither is it simply a recollection of Israel's wrongdoing. Rather, it is a psalm of praise to the Lord, as the first verse suggests, because "his steadfast love endures forever" (v. 1). Psalm 106 is about the history of God's steadfast love toward Israel.

The writer recalls the wickedness of Israel in the land of Egypt in the next paragraph. More importantly, however, he notes that "they did not remember the abundance of [the LORD's] steadfast love" (v. 7). This passage affirms the claim that this psalm is about steadfast love, not sin. The author explains that, despite Israel's forgetfulness, God chooses to save them and remind them of His steadfast love. The twelfth and thirteenth verses of the psalm emphasize the sudden forgetfulness of Israel. First, Israel responds to the love of God by believing His words and singing His praise. In the next verse, the reader finds that, miraculously, Israel has already forgotten the wonderful works of the LORD in delivering them out of Egypt and parting the Red Sea. This thirteenth verse is especially remarkable when considering the context in which it is stated.

Remember, the people of Israel immediately turned away from the LORD after He brought them out of Egypt. There are numerous occasions in which God specifically commanded Israel to remember what the LORD had done in Egypt. In fact, God gives Israel a specific command to remember their slavery in Egypt at least eight separate times in the *Torah* alone. These are just a few examples of this very clear command: Exodus 13:3, Deuteronomy 5:15, Deuteronomy 16:3, Deuteronomy 16:12, Deuteronomy 24:22. Consider that these commands to "remember" are given almost immediately following the deliverance out of Egypt, yet Israel somehow "forgot" all of the LORD's works in Egypt just as quickly.

God repeatedly gives the command to "remember," especially throughout the book of Deuteronomy as Israel apparently continues to forget the works of the LORD and the displays of His steadfast love. The rest of Psalm 106 details the many transgressions of Israel, including craving physical pleasures, jealousy towards Moses and Aaron, idol worship, losing faith in His promise, eating sacrifices offered to the dead, and sacrificing sons and daughters. The root of each of these misdeeds is again emphasized in verses 21-22: "They forgot God, their Savior, who had done great things in Egypt, wondrous works in the land of Ham, and awesome deeds by the Red Sea." God's response to the faithlessness, forgetfulness, and disobedience of Israel is shared in the next verse: "Therefore he said he would destroy them—had not Moses, his chosen one, stood in the breach before him, to turn away his wrath from destroying them" (v. 23). This verse and verse 30, which details Phinehas' intervention on behalf of Israel, are examples of the pattern of Israel's relationship with

God throughout the entire Old Testament.

As Psalm 106 describes, Israel continually turned away from God and acted wickedly, failing to remember the steadfast love of their God. However, God continually responds with love: "Nevertheless, he looked upon their distress, when he heard their cry. For their sake he remembered his covenant and relented according to the abundance of his steadfast love" (v. 44-45). God remembered his covenant, even though Israel forgot. I also love the imagery of the "abundance" of the LORD's steadfast love; He is so overflowing with love that he cannot help but be merciful to His beloved people. This is why God's love is steadfast, never-changing, never-failing: time and again, He planned to treat Israel with complete fairness and destroy them, yet He ultimately decides to have mercy on them.

This is the pattern of the Old Testament: God loves Israel, Israel does not love God back, God (rightfully) decides to destroy Israel, but then He relents. Jesus would come to continue the pattern of intervention marked by Moses and Phinehas and others. He is in fact the complete fulfillment of verse 23, which describes the "chosen one" who would stand in the breach before God, "to turn away his wrath from destroying [Israel]." Not only is Psalm 106 a recollection of past events in which God displayed His steadfast love as a response to Israel's rebellion, but it is also a prophecy of the greatest display of His steadfast love. It is evident that the Old Covenant was not working. Israel kept disobeying, despite the ferocity with which God loved them and sought to bring them into relationship with Him.

Therefore, God the Father sent His one and only Son, the "chosen one," the Messiah *Yeshua*, to be the final sacrifice for Israel. He so yearned for His people to finally understand His steadfast love and respond in accordance with verse 48: "Blessed be the Lord, the God of Israel, from everlasting to everlasting!" However, His love remains steadfast, no matter the response of His beloved children. He knew that some would not receive His love, even after the greatest display of love in Christ's death on the cross. He loved them anyway. This is The Mystery: God showed His steadfast love to Israel in spite of their rebellion; He showed His steadfast love to all by dying on a cross; and He continues to show His steadfast love even to those who reject Him.

THE MYSTERY OF JUDAS
Matthew 26:20-28, Romans 5:8, Titus 2:11 (TLV)

Read these passages, and it may be clear what I am getting at with this chapter. To me, the focal point of this passage in Matthew leading up to the crucifixion is found in verses 27 and 28. Jesus is speaking, but He is not simply addressing Judas. Although He is speaking to all of the twelve, His words are particularly valuable for Judas, whether or not Judas himself realizes it. The rest of the passage leading up to these two verses is critical, yet it can cause us to misinterpret the end of this passage.

Jesus is sitting at the table with the disciples as they are celebrating the Passover. He suddenly shares that one of them will betray Him. The response of the disciples seems strange enough to me. Rather than responding in disbelief, the disciples, one by one, respond, "I'm not the one, am I, Master?" Albeit somewhat confusing, this response reveals that the disciples have a heart to serve Jesus, calling Him Master and showing a sincere desire to not betray Him. However, a few verses later we see the reply of Judas: "I'm not the one, am I, Rabbi?" Perhaps Judas has a different understanding of Jesus than the others. Perhaps he considers Him to be simply a moral teacher, or well-versed Rabbi of the *Torah*, rather than Messiah and Master. Perhaps Judas knows, as Jesus had just proclaimed to his face, that he is committing a great evil in betraying the Messiah. We see that Judas calls Him Rabbi (Teacher), not Master. There is a difference in action and in heart between Judas and the rest of the twelve. Thus, the words and actions of Jesus at the table are quite remarkable.

Jesus breaks the bread and gives it to His disciples. This is where we get to the crux of the story in my opinion, in verses 27 and 28: "And He took a cup, and after giving thanks, He gave to them, saying, 'Drink from it, all of you; for this is My blood of the covenant, which is poured out for many for the removal of sins.'" Jesus says that the cup is representative of the blood of the covenant, the New Covenant in Him. Ezekiel 37:26 is one of multiple passages in the prophets that speak of this new covenant, as the LORD says: "I will cut a covenant of *shalom* with them — it will be an everlasting covenant with them. I will give to them and multiply them. I will set up My Sanctuary among them forever." I could dive deeper into the beauty of this passage and the great promise of the New Covenant. However, for the moment, I want to focus on this passage in Matthew.

Covenants in ancient times were made between people by the shedding of blood. There was a requirement for blood to be shed, in order for a new covenant to be made between God and man. Jesus explains that He is shedding the blood and pouring it out for many for the removal of sins. The blood of Jesus has the power to remove sins for many people. AND HE SAYS TO HIS DISCIPLES, "DRINK FROM IT ALL OF YOU." I usually do not type in all caps, but I want to yell this at you! Do you understand? Jesus tells ALL those with Him at the table, including His betrayer, to drink from the cup representing forgiveness of sins.

As aforementioned, Judas had a different understanding of Jesus, and perhaps he thought he was too far gone. He knew that he was betraying Jesus, and maybe he thought that he could not be forgiven. He had done everything wrong. Jesus declared, "woe to that man by whom the Son of Man is betrayed! It would have been better for that man if he had not been born!" Judas likely felt this way, as the Scripture tells us he later took his own life after betraying Jesus. Jesus knows his heart, and He knows his wrongdoings, and He offers him grace. Titus 2:11 says that "the grace of God has appeared, bringing salvation to all men." As Romans 5:8 declares, God loved us while we were sinners, and He showed us grace. Jesus, in that moment, at the Passover table just before He offered up His life, offered "salvation to all men." He bids us come and drink from the cup. Judas did not deserve it, and we do not deserve it, but that is why it is called grace. This is The Mystery: every person who, like Judas, has betrayed the Messiah by their actions, is offered the cup of grace as an invitation into God's everlasting covenant by the blood of Jesus.

THE MYSTERY OF BARABBAS
Matthew 27:11-26 (TLV)

There is a short message about Barabbas that I love. I have been truly touched by Judah Smith's message "Jesus is Loving Barabbas." Please take the time now to watch this message on YouTube, even if you have already heard it before. It is only a few minutes, and it will be beneficial for your reading of the rest of this chapter.

Judah Smith shares this powerful message about the love of God for Barabbas. It is a beautiful, heart-wrenching sermon for many. There is a reason that I want you to read this passage in the TLV (Tree of Life Version) if possible. The TLV often inserts the original Hebrew words and names used in the Scripture, rather than the Greek or English translations that most of us know. For example, it uses the Hebrew name *Yeshua* instead of the Greek name Jesus. When I first received a TLV Bible, I looked at the back glossary, in which definitions and explanations of more of these Hebrew words are given. I saw the name *Bar-Abba* (Barabbas), which means son of the father. I also saw the name *Yeshua* (Jesus), which means salvation. Then I looked at Matthew 27, where we see the story of Barabbas, or *Bar-Abba*, in relation to the story of the cross. This brought so much greater meaning to the story. Go ahead and read this passage in the TLV before reading the rest of this chapter.

Verses 15 and 16 of Matthew 27 say: "Now during the feast, the governor was accustomed to release to the crowd one prisoner, anyone they wanted. At that time, they had a notorious prisoner, called *Yeshua Bar-Abba*." This is the name of the man we call Barabbas. This is the name of the man that Judah Smith describes as a "rebel," a "murderer," a "bad man." This man has the name "salvation" and "son of the father." What in the world? If what he says is true, then Barabbas does not fit this name. This is so beautiful to me!

I listened to the Judah Smith message again after gaining this understanding, and my favorite part is when he shares this revelation: "When I look at the story, I realize who Barabbas really is. That's me. That's you. That's us." How true! He continues to talk about the love of God in dying for someone like Barabbas, someone so undeserving of His love and so deserving of the punishment. The reason Judah Smith claims that we are each Barabbas is because we are like that man in his actions. We rebelled against God, and God loved us anyway. An even deeper reason that I am like Barabbas is not because I am a sinner, but because, by the grace of God, through faith, I am *Bar-Abba*, a son of the father. For all those who receive the free gift of God's grace, He makes us sons. As stated in Galatians 3:26, "you are all sons of God through trusting in Messiah *Yeshua*." The beauty of the story of Barabbas, or *Bar-Abba*, is not just that God loved a sinful man who may never receive His love. It is wonderful to me because of the meaning of the name of this man and our savior.

The rebel who was set free is named *Yeshua Bar-Abba*. Did the Jews of that day not realize the significance of his name? He has the same name as Jesus (*Yeshua*), meaning "salvation," and he is called "son of the father." That is exactly who Jesus is! Jesus is the Son of God the Father, and He is the one who brings salvation to us. If one were to look at only the names of these two men, they would be essentially the same. If one were to look at the actions of these two men, they would be polar opposites. This truth is so overwhelmingly beautiful to me. As Judah Smith says in his message, God had to treat Jesus like Barabbas so that He could treat Barabbas like Jesus. But wait, there's more! Multiple verses, including Philippians 4:3 and Revelation 3:5, state that NAMES are written in the Book of Life. The name *Bar-Abba*, that I have received, and that all believers have received through the Spirit of adoption in which we have become sons, brings me great joy. It is not our actions that are written in the Book of Life, but our names. All those whose actions would suggest that they are like the rebel Barabbas have become - by the love of God - sons with the name *Bar-Abba*.

It was absolutely necessary for Barabbas to allow Jesus to take his punishment on the cross, but Barabbas had the opportunity to receive the love of God and become a spiritual son of God the Father. We do not know if he fulfilled the meaning of his name to become a son of God. That promise is for us as well, if we would only receive the love of God that takes away our sins and makes us sons.

Judah Smith states in his message that the love of God is scandalous in that He would love a sinful man like Barabbas. I would take it a step further and add this to the meaning of The Mystery. It is so mysterious, so confusing, so awe-inspiring that God would love in such a way. This is The Mystery: God knew our condition as rebellious Barabbas, but He loved us and made us *Bar-Abba*, His sons and daughters.

PART 2

THE MYSTERY OF UNITY
Ephesians 1

There is much to say about Ephesians. I love this book of Scripture, especially because it speaks so much to this topic of The Mystery. It is incredibly important that you read not only the first chapter of Ephesians, but the entire letter. We will begin with chapter one.

A few verses into the chapter, Paul writes quite a lengthy sentence, as he tends to do in his letters. Verses 7-10 happen to be a single sentence in the ESV translation, and this can be difficult to comprehend. I encourage you to slowly break down this section because it contains the first instance of "the mystery" in the letter to the Ephesians. I will simplify this passage as best as I can:

> *God forgave us and redeemed us by His grace, in His wisdom, so that we may know The Mystery of His will. The Mystery is His plan to unite everything in Christ.*

This paraphrase may be helpful, but the entire Scripture is necessary to receive the depths of revelation in this passage.

The main detail of these verses that I want to emphasize is that Christ is meant to bring unity. I am writing this chapter in the midst of a turbulent time in the United States, where I live. Just a few weeks ago, the troublesome death of George Floyd sparked protests, riots, and division across the nation and the world. The panic of COVID-19 has been causing great pain for many, yet the slogans of "we're all in this together" are not exactly supported by the actions of the masses. In a time where unity and brotherly love are absolutely necessary, I see mass destruction, hatred, and political unrest. The overwhelming majority of people are only concerned with their own agendas, even in the Body of Christ. We, as the Church, must be uniting in love, in Christ, rather than causing divisions. This passage in Ephesians 1 is incredibly vital right now and in the coming days.

Later in the first chapter of Ephesians, I find a Scripture that I pray often. Ephesians 1:17-18 is often my prayer for myself and others, as I ask for the Spirit of wisdom and revelation. It is crucial for us to have wisdom and revelation from God to know how to respond to chaotic situations and divisions around us. We also need that which is in verse 15, namely faith in God and "love toward all the saints." I did not realize that this passage would be so potent for the time that I am writing it, as we so desperately need the Body of Christ to unite in love. However, this is a message that we cannot forget. We need wisdom about how to reconcile divisive issues and humility to faithfully love those that are different from us. We continually need to come before God in humility to learn how to love our brothers and sisters. There are specific ways, though, that God's people must be loving, uniting, and reconciling at the time of this writing.

In the midst of the season in which I find myself, the "white church" in particular must be intentional about repenting and reconciling the racial injustices in our nation's history and in the present day. Christians must have unity between races, between black and white and every other ethnicity. We will see later that the primary issue of unity to Paul's audience - the congregation in Ephesus - is that of uniting Jewish and Gentile believers of Messiah. This is still critical in our day, but the issue of unity extends to the need to unite Christians across denominations, political leanings, race, and so on.

In order to bring unity, we must remember those verses I spoke about earlier in Ephesians 7-10. By constantly reflecting on the grace of God, as He has forgiven and redeemed us, we will be capable of walking in such humility necessary to love those around us. By refusing to be filled up with pride and by remembering God's grace, we can show grace to those around us. We can love others instead of being offended by our differences. Whether we are Jewish or not, black or white, Catholic or Protestant, charismatic, evangelical, or what have you, we need to humble ourselves before God and unite as God's people. Then, and only then, can we come into the fullness of God's purpose for His people. This is The Mystery: Christ came to reconcile us unto God and empower us to bring reconciliation and unity into the world around us.

REMEMBER THE MYSTERY
Ephesians 2:11-22

There is a pattern in the *Tanakh* that I love. Although the exact wording changes, God repeatedly instructs Israel to "remember." What does He tell them to remember? He tells them to remember their slavery. Deuteronomy 5:15 is one of many examples where the LORD speaks about this to Israel: "You shall remember that you were a slave in the land of Egypt, and the LORD your God brought you out from there with a mighty hand and an outstretched arm. Therefore the LORD your God commanded you to keep the Sabbath day." What a curious and incredibly important statement. Let us discuss the importance of such remembrance.

Recently, due to ever-increasing racial tensions, there has been news about multiple locations in the United States tearing down statues of former Confederate army leaders. Somewhere, however, I saw one person's opinion that keeping up the statues is helpful for people to be reminded of our nation's history. Many people want to forget such a horrific history, but I'm not sure that will do us any good. We must remember where we were, so that we can appreciate where we are now and consider where we need to go.

Israel is commanded multiple times to remember Egypt, but this specific instance in Deuteronomy 5 comes at an important moment. The Israelites are at Mount Sinai, after the exodus from Egypt but before the entrance into the Promised Land. Israel was commanded to remember their slavery in Egypt because God brought them out. Israel was also commanded to remember their slavery in Egypt so they would believe that God would bring them forward into the promise. Again, Israel needed to remember from where God had brought them, so that they would appreciate where God was still bringing them.

The "remember" command for Israel is regarding their slavery in Egypt. The Gentile equivalent to this command is found in Ephesians 2. In verses 11 and 12, God commands the Gentile church at Ephesus, as well as every Gentile believer, to remember: "remember that you were at that time separate from Christ, alienated from the commonwealth of Israel and strangers to the covenants of promise, having no hope and without God in the world" (Ephesians 2:12). Geez, Paul (apparently there's some dispute on how to spell "geez." If you don't like the way that I spelled it, too bad). Did you read that? What a terrible thing to remember. But God is reminding the Gentiles of what they used to be. They once were strangers. They once were people with no hope. They once were without God. But not anymore!

This passage in Ephesians 2 is an excellent summary of The Mystery. Read it closely. Find all the details of The Mystery: the good news that the wall that separated Jew and Gentile has been broken. See that Jews and Gentiles have both been reconciled to God and made into One New Man. Don't read only what I've written. That's not the point of this book. If you haven't been reading the Scripture passages, go back and read them. What I want to emphasize in this chapter, is this one aspect of The Mystery: we must "remember" The Mystery.

I don't know for certain, but I would suspect that the majority of my audience consists of Gentile believers in Christ, or non-Jewish Christians. This is where I challenge that specific audience to Remember The Mystery. A major reason for writing this book is that we aren't really experiencing what Ephesians 2:11-22 describes. Jews and Gentiles are meant to be "one new man" in the body of Christ. But many Jews do not have a relationship with Christ. Many Jews consider Christians to be judgmental and hypocritical. Many Jews have not heard the gospel, The Mystery of the Scriptures they read. Due to the pride and selfishness of "Christians" throughout the ages, the script has been completely flipped. Paul, a Jewish member of the largely Jewish Body of Christ, wrote to Gentile believers in the book of Ephesians. He wrote, preached, and prayed for the Gentiles to be welcomed into the body, bringing unity and fulfilling the Scriptures. Now, the Gentile Church must return the favor and welcome the Jews into the household of God, under Christ.

There is another "remember" command given many times to the people of Israel, and it is actually referenced at the end of Deuteronomy 5:15. It is the command to "remember the Sabbath." The reason that God commanded them to remember and keep the Sabbath day is so that they would remember how God delivered them from the land of Egypt. The Sabbath is another issue that I would like to bring before the modern Gentile Church. We have largely lost a reverence for God, a reverence for the commands of the *Torah*, and a reverence for rest. Under the New Covenant, we are no longer bound by the legalism of the Old Covenant. However, some statutes of the Old Covenant have been neglected, namely the practice of Sabbath. This was a command that God gave for the sake of His people. Therefore, practice the Sabbath. Take a day of rest each week to enjoy our King. I prefer to practice the Sabbath as Jews do, as an act of unity with my Jewish brothers in Christ, by resting from sundown on Friday to sundown on Saturday. This is one simple act that honors God, strengthens our spirits, and helps us remember The Mystery of unity between Jew and Gentile.

I stated that the focus of this chapter is meant to be on remembering The Mystery. Ephesians 2:11-22 explains very well what it is, as it says that Christ creates "in himself one new man in place of [Jew and Gentile]" (v. 15). This is The Mystery. Now remember it.

THE MYSTERY OF CHRIST
Ephesians 3:1-13

I am beginning to write this chapter without really knowing what I'm going to write. My heart is heavy with the weight and beauty of these thirteen verses. It is so vital that you read it carefully. There is a reason that Paul wrote about this topic, by the influence of the Spirit. It is heavy on my heart, and it is my role to bring this Scripture to your attention, rather than merely talk about it.

I titled this chapter The Mystery of Christ because it was that line in Ephesians 3:4 that sparked the idea for this book. In fact, I want to tell you to really dive into verses 4-6 of Ephesians 3. At the same time, the whole section is great, so I really want you to dive into all of it. Even so, Ephesians 3:4-6 is a great explanation of The Mystery. Verse 3 is incredibly important as well, because Paul explains that The Mystery was made known to him by revelation. Without revelation from the Holy Spirit, we cannot truly grasp the truths presented here. It is crucial that we each humble ourselves to be taught by the Scriptures and the Spirit.

I love The Mystery of Christ. Jesus was truly a mystery to many people while He walked on the earth. As Paul explains, He was even a mystery to people of the past who heard prophecies about Him. They knew a Messiah would come, but what would He do? Some thought He would lead a rebellion to overthrow the Roman Empire and bring a King back to David's throne in Jerusalem. Amazingly, The Mystery explained by Paul does not seem to be about Israel at all. He was supposed to be the Messiah and King of the Jews. Jesus himself explained to a Gentile woman that He "was sent only to the lost sheep of the house of Israel" (Matthew 15:24). This is why it is a mystery. This is why it is so confusing, so shocking that the Gentiles would be welcomed in as children themselves. This is why Paul says, "This mystery is that the Gentiles are fellow heirs, members of the same body, and partakers of the promise in Christ Jesus through the gospel" (Ephesians 3:6). A scandalous claim in the ears of many Jews at that time.

Now get ready for some Greek. I am no expert in the Greek language. I have never studied it, but I am going to talk about it because it might prove helpful to our understanding of The Mystery. We've heard some good stuff about The Mystery so far, but let's move onto Ephesians 3:9-10. These two verses give us some insight into the reason for knowing and sharing The Mystery. We know this because of these two words at the beginning of verse 10: "so that." The part following "so that" is the reason for the part before "so that." Paul states in verse 9 that he is bringing The Mystery to light for everyone. And, as explained in verse 10, the reason that Paul brings The Mystery to light is for the wisdom of God to be made known "to the rulers and authorities in the heavenly places." I know there was kind of a lot of buildup, but this is where we are bringing out the Greek.

This is what I did in my limited knowledge. I was writing this chapter on my computer, so I went to Google and searched up "Ephesians 3:10 Greek." I looked at the Greek words to better understand what this verse means because I was a little confused when I first read it. Why is The Mystery meant to be brought to light so that "the rulers and authorities in the heavenly places" would know God's wisdom? Therefore, I looked at the Greek words for "rulers," "authorities," and "heavenly places."

First off, I found that the Greek word used here for "heavenly places" is found only in the book of Ephesians. We find the word *epouraniois* five times in Ephesians, in the following verses: Ephesians 1:3, Ephesians 1:20, Ephesians 2:6, Ephesians 3:10, and Ephesians 6:12. The first three verses talk about being in heavenly places with Christ. Ephesians 3:10 is of course the verse we are looking at. Ephesians 6:12 was most helpful to me because it also spoke about rulers or authorities.

I also looked at the Greek word, *exousiais*, meaning "authorities" in this text. It was only found in the New Testament in two other places, referring to earthly authorities. I didn't find this very helpful. Besides, Ephesians 6:12 had the word "rulers," not "authorities" in the version I was reading.

I found that the Greek word, *archais*, which is "rulers" in this passage, is in the New Testament only three other times. Two of those times it is translated "corners" in the story of Peter's vision in Acts 10. So far, the Greek study was not very beneficial to me. At this point, my deficiencies in Greek may become even more evident. The website has links to the right of the page with similar Greek words used elsewhere in the Bible. I discovered that the Greek word, *archas*, is the word for "rulers" in Ephesians 6:12. (Due to my non-expertise in Greek, I am not sure if this is entirely relevant. I am okay with that. The purpose of this book is to share my discoveries about the Bible and God's purpose, encouraging you to read the Bible and allow God to teach you as well.) Thus, this Greek word confirmed for me that there are similarities between Ephesians 3:10 and Ephesians 6:12, in that "the rulers and authorities in the heavenly places" are wicked spiritual forces, aka satan and the demonic forces.

The point that I am getting at here is my explanation of

Ephesians 3:9-10. It states that The Mystery is brought to light, so that the church may show the demons the wisdom of God. It makes sense to me. Think about this: they must have been so confused when Jesus rose from that grave. I'm not saying that satan and the demonic forces are stupid. But they are most certainly prideful. And pride can be very blinding. They thought they won, but they were blind to the fact that God had won. They must have been confused as to why Jesus would die on the cross. They didn't realize that God was planning on redeeming not only Israel, but the entire world, Gentiles included!

God reveals The Mystery to us so that we can know the manifold wisdom of God, and so that, through us, even the enemy can know God's wisdom. God had a plan this whole time. He's like a chess grandmaster. The enemy is thinking he's going to win, but he has no idea about God's secret weapon. God reveals His wisdom to humble everyone else, prove He's the boss, and then drop the mic in satan's face. Epic.

I wrote kind of a lot in this chapter because I made some interesting discoveries. I want to end with the reminder that all of this is about Christ. It is The Mystery of Christ. It is the mysterious, amazing, loving act of His sacrifice on the cross that it is all about. There is so much in Ephesians 3 about the depths of this mystery, but that is the foundation of it all. Because it is worded so well, spoken by the breath of God, I will conclude by quoting Ephesians 3:6. This is The Mystery: "the Gentiles are fellow heirs, members of the same body, and partakers of the promise in Christ Jesus through the gospel."

THE MYSTERY OF GOD'S PEOPLE
Romans 9-10

There is much to be said about this passage. These two chapters are so incredibly vital to the message of The Mystery. If you have not read them in full, I urge you to do so. If you have, do it again. There is a great deal of revelation to be found in chapters nine and ten of Paul's letter to the Christians in Rome. My prayer is that you would dive into these passages with humility to receive revelation from Holy Spirit. That being said, I want to focus on The Mystery of God's People in this chapter.

I say this because it really does seem like a mystery as to who would be considered God's People. Israel have always been the chosen people of God. Is this still the case, or are the Jews and Gentiles now jointly considered God's people? It seems a little bit confusing. On the one hand, Paul quotes Hosea and claims that the Gentiles — those who were not God's people — are now God's people. He also states that "there is no distinction between Jew and Greek" (Romans 10:12).

However, why would he take the time in Romans 9 to discuss election, to discuss the treasures that belong to the Israelites, to discuss how God chose Jacob (Israel) instead of his brother Esau? It appears as if Israel plays a major role in God's story, and the Jews are set apart in His eyes. Here is another point to consider: I have heard testimonies of Jews who realized the power of their heritage and identification with Israel. Does their Jewish heritage matter at all, or are Jews and Gentiles the same? We need to understand why the Hebrew roots of the Christian faith matter. We need to understand why there is also no distinction between Jews and non-Jews. It is a fascinating dichotomy to dissect, and we need to seek revelation from God to better understand it.

The LORD has revealed to me that the reason why "there is no distinction between Jew and Greek" (Romans 10:12) is because of the following verse. There is no distinction in that both Jew and Greek may be saved by calling on the name of the LORD. This does not mean that Jews and Gentiles are the same. God does not show favoritism, but He has called Jew and Gentile to different purposes in His Kingdom.

Israel are the people of God's inheritance. God chose Israel to give to them the treasures that Paul speaks of in Romans 9: "the adoption, the glory, the covenants" (v. 4), etc. Now, Gentiles have been welcomed in, that they may share in this inheritance. Therefore, there is no longer any distinction between Jew and Gentile, as both have received salvation in Christ.

There is a reason, however, that I want to emphasize the Gentiles *sharing* in the inheritance of the Jews. It may merely seem like semantics, but elsewhere it is said that the gospel is the power of God for salvation "to the Jew first and also to the Greek" (Romans 1:16). In the ministry of *Yeshua*, He made clear that He came to save the lost children of Israel. The reason why I make this point is to remind believers of our heritage.

The modern church largely consists of Gentiles who do not fully appreciate the Hebrew roots of the faith. The early church entirely consisted of Jews. It is vital for believers to recognize, as Paul did, the love that God has for Israel. His response to the revelation of The Mystery is found in Romans 9:1-3 and Romans 10:1. Paul understood that, although Jews and Gentiles are now

One New Man in Messiah *Yeshua*, God chose Israel for a reason, and He desires for all of Israel to be saved. My heart longs for the Body of Christ to come into alignment with the heart of the Father in prayer and yearning for the salvation of Israel.

The last couple nuggets of revelation that I want to share are in Romans 10:14-17. Paul reminds his audience, the Gentile believers in Rome, of the importance of preaching the gospel to the Jews. This is still a crucial message to non-Jewish Christians of today. I believe there is also a bit of a hint as to how we are meant to preach the gospel to the Jews. A reference to Isaiah 53:1 is found in Romans 10:16. I have heard many Jewish stories that testify to the power of the Messianic prophecy in Isaiah 53. The Holy Spirit has often worked mightily to open the eyes of Jewish people as they discover that *Yeshua* of Nazareth clearly fulfills the prophecy of the Messiah in their Scriptures. We must have an understanding of the *Tanakh* to be able to effectively share the gospel with the Jews. My encouragement to believers, both Jew and Gentile, is to seek the Father's heart for the people of Israel, as we have been so blessed to join into Israel's inheritance from the Father.

God, in His grace, has provided both Jew and Gentile the opportunity to join in His story, The Mystery. We are blessed to experience the beauty of Jew and Gentile united in Messiah *Yeshua*. This is The Mystery: God's people are Israel, but now, through Jesus, all of humanity can be His people as well.

THE MYSTERY OF JEALOUSY
Romans 11

We have spent some time discussing The Mystery, and I pray that you have come to understand it better. We have dove into multiple Scripture passages that offer us insight into the relationship between Jews and Gentiles in God's plan. We have looked at the role that *Yeshua* has in reconciling that relationship. The other parts of Scripture are incredibly important in understanding The Mystery, but Romans 11 may just be the focal point of it all.

I say this because this chapter does so well in summarizing The Mystery. We just looked at Romans 9-10. Those two chapters prepare us in an immense way for the power of Romans 11. You need to look at this chapter a few times, with humility to receive revelation from Holy Spirit. I am going to talk about a few details that really stand out to me.

Verses 11-14 are super important, especially for Paul's Gentile audience. For Gentile readers of this book, it is still very necessary for us to take note of these verses. This section is why I call it The Mystery of Jealousy.

Jealousy always seems to get a bad rap. It's a sin, right? Isn't jealousy bad? If jealousy is a sin, though, then why is God jealous? Most of us are probably pretty familiar with the Ten Commandments. But right in the midst of these famous commands from the LORD, He says the following about Himself: "I the LORD your God am a jealous God" (Exodus 20:5). The

Mystery of Jealousy is continued in Romans 11:11-14, as it is implied that both God and Paul want to make the Jews jealous. Why would they desire for the Jews to sin, if jealousy is in fact a sin? This is why I wonder if jealousy really is a sin. God cannot sin, but the Bible says He is jealous and wants His people to become jealous. There is an important distinction to be made here, and I will pose a question to help us understand: what is it that we are jealous for?

If you look back at the context of Exodus 20 and the Ten Commandments, you will find God's answer to this question. God tells the people that He is jealous for them, as He is commanding them not to turn to idols. Israel could not have earned this kind of love, but God is telling them, in effect: "all I want is you and for you to only want Me." That is why God wants Israel to become jealous, and thus why the Gentiles were welcomed in. Paul expresses this truth throughout Romans 11.

The goal of The Mystery is to make the Jews jealous, so that they would be saved. Paul uses the metaphor of an olive tree to explain that the Jews are God's people, the olive tree. The Gentiles are the wild olive shoot that was grafted into the tree. He explains that Israel's disobedience enabled the Gentiles to be grafted in. He uses this metaphor to say that essentially the script has been flipped.

The Jews were always God's people. They disobeyed and were cut off from Him. Through Messiah *Yeshua*, the Gentiles could be brought near to God. Now, through the Gentiles, the Jews are meant to be brought back to God as well. This is the whole point of Paul's message to the Gentile believers in Rome.

He says that when the Jews are grafted back into the olive tree, it makes the tree stronger and greater. He says that Gentiles are meant to turn the Jews back to God, to receive mercy just as we have received mercy. He says that the full inclusion of the Jews is greater than riches for the Gentiles!

There is a great deal of doctrine in this chapter, but what are the practical steps that Paul gives? First off, he tells the Gentile audience about his role — as a Jew — in The Mystery. Paul tells them that he is a minister to the Gentiles, so that his fellow Jews make become jealous and be saved. Therefore, my first suggestion to you is to ask God what your role is in The Mystery.

We know that unity between Jew and Gentile in the church will bring forth much fruit. However, verse 25 states that "the fullness of the Gentiles" must come in for all of Israel to be saved. Evidently, not everyone is called to primarily preach the gospel to the Jews. The gospel also must be shared with Gentiles, and other people have a calling to participate in strengthening the faith of both Jewish and Gentile believers. As far as I understand, though, not many are preaching the gospel to the Jews or working to reconcile the relationship between Jew and Gentile. Paul was confident in his role in this process. The first step for us in responding to The Mystery is to ask God about our role

Second, Paul admonishes Gentile believers to turn from pride. Twice he commands it in Romans 11: "do not be arrogant toward the branches" (verse 18) and "do not become proud, but fear" (verse 20). Similarly, Paul tells them not to be wise in their own sight. You may notice that this was the issue that caused the Jews to fall. Paul writes that the Jews had "eyes that would not see" (Romans 11:8). Paul is continually reminding the Gentile believers to be humble and seek wisdom from God. He warns them that they may be cut off for their pride, just as the Jews had been. Therefore, the second step for us is to walk in humility before God, as well as toward others, both Jew and Gentile.

Finally, Paul closes chapter 11 with worship to God. He praises

God for His wisdom and kindness, displayed in The Mystery. God has shown His love to us in this marvelous, mysterious plan. He has shown His love to both Jew and Gentile, as both may be reconciled to Him. The final step in response to The Mystery, as found in Romans 11, is to worship God for His grace toward us as Jew and Gentile, and for the wonderful invitation to participate in His plan.

There is so much depth to this chapter of Romans, particularly in Paul's explanation of The Mystery. The Mystery of Jealousy is meant to bring Gentiles and Jews into a united olive tree in Messiah. This is The Mystery: "a partial hardening has come upon Israel, until the fullness of the Gentiles has come in" (verse 25), so that Israel may be saved, and Jew and Gentile may be blessed.

THE MYSTERY OF HONOR
Romans 12

I recently heard my friend, Alex, preach on Romans 12 and honor. The central point of Romans 12 is the tenth verse, which instructs us to "outdo one another in showing honor." Alex spoke about the importance of honoring one another, despite our differences. He reminded me that the twelfth chapter of Romans is where Paul tells his audience what to do about the awesome doctrine preceding it. I want to explain that further.

You see, honor is crucial to The Mystery. I discussed the significance of Romans 9-11 in the context of The Mystery. We talked about how Paul brings together all this teaching about the Jews and Gentiles within The Mystery. But then what does he say? He instructs his Gentile audience to honor the Jews.

Paul uses the previous chapters to explain the gospel. He tells the Gentile believers that they are free from sin because of Christ's sacrifice. He tells them that Israel are the people of the promise. He tells them that God decides, however, to include the Gentiles and make them also His people. He tells them that they were chosen to make the Jews jealous, so that Israel would be saved, along with all nations. How are they meant to respond?

"I appeal to you, therefore, brothers, by the mercies of God, to present your bodies as a living sacrifice, holy and acceptable to God, which is your spiritual worship" (Romans 12:1).

You see that "therefore" right there? I always hear people say that whenever you read a "therefore" in the Bible, you need to ask what it's there for. This is a good idea, but it isn't always applied correctly. What people tend to do is go back a few verses to find what was said just prior. This is a big problem that arises when a lot of people read the Scriptures. They too often look at passages in isolation. I understand that it is usually difficult to read an entire book of the Bible in one sitting. I probably wouldn't recommend reading all of Romans at once. That's not what I am saying. It is not necessary to read the letter all at once, but it is necessary to recognize that the letter was likely written all at once. Therefore, we are going to understand that Paul's use of "therefore" is not just referencing the previous few verses.

As a matter of fact, he is admonishing the Gentile believers in Rome to humble themselves before God, in submission to the Father's purposes for Israel. There is a great deception infiltrating some Christian circles, the idea called replacement theology. This theological idea claims that the Church has replaced Israel. Thus, prophecies about Israel in the Bible would actually be about the Church. As far as I know, most Christians seem to refute this belief. However, it may have infiltrated our thinking enough that we are lacking honor for Israel and their role in God's plan.

Paul teaches the believers about the importance of different gifts and unity in the Body of Christ. He instructs the Gentiles to not think of themselves more highly than they ought. He gave the same instruction in Romans 11:18, as he tells them to not be arrogant. Another very important commandment in chapter 12 is to "not be conformed to this world" (verse 2). The Gentile Church failed massively in this regard.

As more and more Gentiles were welcomed into the family of God, they eventually forsook the Jewish roots of the faith, replacing them with worldly practices. The biblical feasts were replaced with Christmas and Easter. The Sabbath day was replaced with Sunday. In my opinion, it is not such a big deal for modern Christians to worship on Sunday and celebrate Christmas and Easter. However, at the time, these were intentional acts to remove Jewish influences from a new religion, Christianity. The foundation of Christianity was a Jewish Messiah, from the Jewish people, fulfilling the prophecies of the Jewish Scriptures. The Jews were pushed out of the Church.

Paul tells the Gentiles that the Jews are crucial to God's plan for the world, so they are meant to honor them. And they fail to do so. Therefore, my encouragement in this chapter is to honor others, particularly for Gentile Christians to honor the Jews and Israel. Once again, Paul uses this chapter to share practical ways for the Church to honor others, so I would encourage you to again look at the instructions of Romans 12 in the context of reconciling the relationship between Jew and Gentile.

Here are some additional ways for today's Gentile Church to honor the nation of Israel and Jews around the world. Search out local synagogues and visit them. I am blessed to have a Messianic synagogue in my city. This is a Jewish synagogue of people who believe in *Yeshua* as the Messiah. Visiting a Messianic synagogue, or any Jewish synagogue near you, can help restore relations between Christians and Jews. Joining Jewish believers in celebrating the biblical feasts is a great way to unite under biblical principles, rather than mere Christian traditions. Praying blessings upon Israel, giving financially to Jewish ministries, and seeking God's heart for unity are also great ideas.

The idea of this book was to dive into this topic of The Mystery because it is pretty complicated. It has many layers and divisive subjects within it. There are people who have different viewpoints on Israel and Christianity and all of these important conversations.

It is important, however, to recognize that The Mystery certainly involves the role of Israel in God's purposes. It is important that we understand that Romans 9-11 contains a lot of doctrine about Jews and Gentiles. And the twelfth chapter of Romans tells us what to do about this doctrine. This is The Mystery: God chose many different people, both Jew and Gentile, for different purposes in His Kingdom, and His Kingdom is advanced as we honor each other.

THE GLORY OF THE MYSTERY
Colossians 1:24-2:8

Before we go any further into studying this passage, we need to perhaps start in the middle. In Colossians 2, we find that in Christ "are hidden all the treasures of wisdom and knowledge" (v. 3). There is a great deal of important theology that I have brought up in this book, some of which may be difficult to understand or receive. It is important to remember that all the treasures of wisdom and knowledge are not hidden in me, nor in you. Rather, we must seek wisdom and knowledge from Christ concerning all things, including The Mystery. In fact, as this passage states, that is The Mystery.

The Mystery is multi-faceted. However, its foundation is simply Christ. This passage states that The Mystery is "Christ in you, the hope of glory" (Col. 1:27), and it is "Christ, in whom are hidden all the treasures of wisdom and knowledge" (Col. 2:2-3). We must remember this core truth, even as we dive into the depths of The Mystery. The truth is simple, but there are still greater depths that we can find in it.

Another piece of information that may help us understand this passage about The Mystery is actually found elsewhere in the letter to the Colossians. At the end of Paul's letter, he gives this instruction: "And when this letter has been read among you, have it also read in the church of the Laodiceans; and see that you also read the letter from Laodicea" (Col. 4:16). It is helpful for us to understand the relationship between these two cities, Colossae and Laodicea. It was not uncommon for communication to be shared between the two cities, as they were only about 10 miles apart. (As an illustration for my friends living in the Cincinnati area, that is about the same distance between Blue Ash and Mason.) This is similar to a modern-day church having multiple campuses in a city. There is a letter sent to Colossae, so that it may be shared with Laodicea as well, just as two church campuses may share sermons.

The reason why I am giving this contextual information is because of what many of us know Laodicea for. Laodicea is the famous "lukewarm" congregation in Revelation 3. I am proposing that the message to Colossae and Laodicea in Paul's letter may help us understand the message that John gives to the church in the book of Revelation. Similarly, Paul writes a letter to the Ephesians in Ephesus, and John shares a message from God to Ephesus in Revelation 2. Both Ephesians and Colossians are included in The Mystery, as they are letters revealing The Mystery to Gentile believers. I encourage you to look at Revelation 2:1-7 and Revelation 3:14-22 in relation to The Mystery and the letters to the Ephesians and Colossians.

I have given quite a bit of background information in this chapter. This is the final chapter of The Mystery, but the journey does not end here. I am still learning about the intricacies of God's Mystery, and I encourage you to seek the same. As we wrap up this book and continue to learn about The Mystery in our personal study of Scripture, it is vital that we remember the information I shared in this chapter. That is why I took the time to remind us that Christ is the source of wisdom and knowledge and that context and other Bible passages will help us understand His Word.

Finally, I now want to share the revelation that stood out to me from this section of Colossians. It states that God revealed His hidden Mystery to the saints. It states that The Mystery is Christ in us. It states that there are riches of glory among the Gentiles because of The Mystery. This is a big deal!

The Jews knew about the glory of God, at least to an extent. The glory of God dwelt in the tabernacle of Moses, and then in the temple in the Holy of Holies. On the cross, the veil of the temple was torn, providing the Jews access by the Spirit to the Holy of Holies. On Pentecost, the Jewish disciples of Christ experienced this glory in the baptism of the Spirit. But now they have heard The Mystery that there are greater riches of glory among the Gentiles. Part of going "from glory to glory" (2 Cor. 3:18) is found in the unity of Jew and Gentile in Christ.

Paul understands this mystery, so he states that he is toiling with all his energy to make known The Mystery to others, that everyone may be "mature in Christ" (Col. 1:29). We must long for this unity and maturity in Christ, so that we may experience the greater glory. Thus, my instruction is the same as Paul's.

Paul instructs us that wisdom and knowledge are found in Christ, and he warns the church twice to not be taken captive by arguments and worldly wisdom (Col. 2:4, 8). Therefore, the encouragement is to abide in Christ, to "walk in him" (v. 6). It is my encouragement for you as well.

There are great riches in the glory of The Mystery that we can partake in. Christ himself is the hope of glory in The Mystery, but there are greater depths to be found in the unity of Christ between Jew and Gentile. This is The Mystery: Christ is in us — both Jew and Gentile — and He is the hope of glory.

THE MYSTERY CONCLUSION

I like to ask questions of others, and I like to leave room for others to ask questions of me when having conversation. The Mystery may be a complicated subject. My mission in this book was to introduce the idea of The Mystery and encourage others to search it out for themselves. That being said, you might have questions. You might have comments. You might agree with what I have shared. You might completely disagree with every word in this book. If you want to ask questions or further discuss the contents of this book, reach out to me here:

tyler.witten.book@gmail.com

I urge you to respond to The Mystery in some way. As Paul shared in the letter to the Colossians, he is toiling to make The Mystery known. We have a responsibility to each toil in our own manner as ministers of reconciliation and members of Christ's body. Certainly, continue to dive into the Bible and seek out The Mystery. I could have added much more to this book, but that would have kind of defeated the point. We have all of eternity to discover the mysteries of God, so this book could have never sufficed to explain it. Searching out the depths of our Creator is what our lives are about: "It is the glory of God to conceal things, but the glory of kings is to search things out" (Proverbs 25:2). If you make any great discoveries, feel free to share your findings with me through email.

Perhaps you are interested in learning more about the Hebraic roots of the Bible, Messianic Judaism, or Israel. The following are resources that I enjoy and trust:

- Messianic Jewish Family Bible (TLV)

    Bible that I use often; uses transliterated Hebrew words such as *Yeshua, Elohim, shalom*; includes the *Shema* and Aaronic Blessing in Hebrew; very interesting Bible translation

- One New Man Bible

    Bible translation intended to reflect the original Hebrew and Greek meaning; includes Glossary with in-depth explanation of Hebrew festivals, customs, etc.

- *Born a Jew…Die a Jew* by Yohanna Chernoff

    The story of Martin Chernoff, a pioneer in Messianic Judaism, as written by his wife; very powerful story; insight into the revival of the 1970s

- *Your People Shall Be My People* by Don Finto

    At the time of this writing, I have only read some of this book, but it is incredible; reveals greater depths of the history and significance of Israel in God's purposes

- BEMA Discipleship Podcast

    Wonderfully in-depth podcast about the eastern, Jewish perspective on the Scriptures; very helpful for Western Christians to understand the Bible

- A Jew and a Gentile Discuss

    This podcast is relatively new to me; a Jewish believer in

Messiah and a Gentile believer in Messiah discuss many issues about Messianic Judaism, Israel, and related topics

- oneforisrael.org

    Website for Messianic Jewish ministry seeking salvation of Israel; shares fascinating "I Met Messiah" testimonies of Jews believing in *Yeshua*

Finally, I just want to thank you for reading this book. This was a cool project for me to work on the past couple of years. I wrote this book for you, to challenge and inspire. I hope that you enjoyed it. Be blessed.

ABOUT THE AUTHOR

Tyler Wittenbrook is a writer, a leader, and an intercessor in Cincinnati, Ohio. He is passionate about the Word of God and the people of Israel. His great desire is to be a doorkeeper in the House of God, seeking the face of the LORD and inviting people into the House.

www.ingramcontent.com/pod-product-compliance
Lightning Source LLC
Chambersburg PA
CBHW070105100426
42743CB00012B/2652